Sunland Park Poems

by

Elsa Frausto and Alice Pero

Sunland Park Poems

Copyright © 2017 by Shabda Press

All rights reserved. No part of this book may be reproduced or transmitted in any form or by any means without written permission of the author.

Photo credits:
Cover and other tree photo, Alice Pero
Photo of poets: Ander Frausto

ISBN: 978-0-9915772-6-2

Published by Shabda Press
Pasadena, CA 91107
www.shabdapress.com

PREFACE

Two Sunland/Tujunga poets decided to write poems in Sunland Park, meeting on Tuesday mornings on warm spring days under the sheltering branches of towering pine and live oak. Eventually a book began to form and is dedicated to the park with its visitors and quasi-residents, squirrels, sparrows and one lone saxophone player. A certain bond was formed amongst the poets, the trees, the people of the Senior Center, morning strollers and even the dust blowing about in air which turned increasingly hot as months went on. This large park breathes life in and out and the wind coming from the San Gabriel Foothills pulled poems out of the poets as it scoured the paths. The spirit of Sunland Park and its people lives in these poems.

The Editors

ELSA'S POEMS

The poem dances.
Fact, no simile or metaphor.
It's the youngest limb on that tree.
There it goes- my metaphor
can't help itself.
At 10 am, it becomes a boat
swaying on the calm sea
and here's the fisherman,
a darker silhouette on the horizon.

It fits here.
Diastole and systole.
Sometimes I forget to breathe.
Then I remember
how heart and lungs
or a boat and its oars
need each other
to fall asleep.

It's when the intimation of a poem begins with bird song
that I have to listen.

Breeze at my back
not pushing me
it lets me stay
and we have a conversation

Footsteps on a sandy pathway
I try not to look

I could be somewhere else
but I am here
while you sit
in silence
next to me

Everything sings
even the flagpole
has a beat and a ring

Twenty five years to belong
I measure time by the crop
of this season's oranges

Saxophone plays, moves the still air,
brushes around palm trees, then stops.
Other sounds take over-
a car's horn, someone's voice at 11 am,
distance also a voyage of consonants and vowels.
Only two miles away from home but further.
Good to travel like this
without effort, through sound and air.

Alice sits in sunlight.
Green grass around her
like an island.
An ant crawls up her leg
and not until her bare arm
does she notice it.
Let's see how far it goes.
And if A. blows it away,
I'll keep it
in these lines.
Come, ant, ascend the poem.

Horizon where mountain meets the sky—
eyes settle there.
Wait until the past and present reconcile.
Or until the crow's cawing lits you down.

Fire

I'm cold. To sit by a fire pit now
amid the tall pines
and your face looking up
all dressed in light.

Another story about fire

Once I heard about a house
cold in the winter
and for fuel, books were burnt.
I wonder how many were enough
on a long winter's night.

White page stares back.
Only for a second.
Then the pen
writes and changes everything.
But if change is the nature of things,
does it matter?

There are people I want
to meet
not know
as if in passing
some secret wink
spells a name
the same a mirror holds
and we recognize each other

A poem
        with two doors,
one, to come in, the other
        to leave.

Three windows,
        one for the sun,
one for the moon and the third,
to see you walking down the road.

New York, London, Paris
and the list goes on, L.A.
and here we are. Three women
writing in the park
with our backs to the sun,
face to the breeze,
each in ourselves and out there.
Really, here we are.

How it changes!
All it takes is a man
walking a few steps
towards the water fountain
to take sips of what he needs.
And someone looking at him.

Waiting is like this
Sunlight on my eyes
and at my back
some warmth
like a secret
in plain sight
we all share
Like the shadow
of an inclined head
and a hand
that writes
what it didn't know
a minute ago
Discovery is quick
Waiting is slow
In between, the crow,
announces its arrival

I want to give that palm tree a frond cut
return its regal shape
It's such a young one, after all

In the broken notes of his saxophone,
a man writes a life.
This one says- I practice here
because I can't at home.
If they are broken, well, so is my life.
But I still come to the park
and my body curves in the shade it makes.

Dust settles faster than sand.
This is sand as the wind
lifts it, curls the grains
on their way down.
And they land.
I think this quiet
won't be for long.
Uncertainty is an island
with land on the other side.
For now, I live on this island.

It's a small word, fits in the corner of an eye, the fold of skin where upper and lower arm meet, where night and sleep meet and lull it to sleep. We carry it everywhere, old baggage or new, or it carries us like babies we are. We learn to conjugate our life with it.
It's the same word for you and me. Sometimes we forget.

I was going to say- brown-
until your hazel eyes looked at me.

Nothing is translatable
unless
nada es traducible
and the words take you
where sound and meaning
conjugate
y las palabras te llevan
adonde el sonido y lo que dice
se conjuga
like agua/water
and you are thirsty for them
after the letters roll out
y tienes sed de ellas
después de que las letras ruedan
from your mouth
y se pierden en el mundo
and they get lost in the world
de tu boca

If I don't lift my eyes,
the path is open
with the play of light and shadow.
And when eyes look up
into the depth of green pines,
I can almost see where
smell of dry pine needles
meets the breeze above.
It seems we live outside,
inside and within borders.
There's enough periphery
around that tree for me
to join in the dance.

Sunlight through clouds
Then only one
covers the sun
and that's all it takes

Outsider moon
silver
with borrowed
light
Your costume
becomes you
Lend me
your light

———

Conversation
like a map
spread out
on a table.
Look at this island.
I'd like to go there.
When the next ship sails,
I wonder what clothes
to take,
what language is spoken.
Do the ocean currents
invite the swimmer?

———

Thank you to the hands
that once in time
built that stone wall.
Sometimes it's easy

to be in the world.
Why conjugate?

The poem is for me
while others spy.
Be my other.

Intransit

I walk
moon slides behind
palm trees
suspended breath
of sky

Attempt to cross the world
eyes closed.
Let music guide my steps.
I carry the profile of mountains
drawn on my forehead

There's a moment
when eyes
sink
in the flight
of two birds
when my being
doesn't know
it ends here
and becomes
breath in the eyes
round trip
and then one way

An invitation
to be
when the afternoon
ends
its abbreviated walk
of fish
in the gray sea
of the sky

Same sun
               like moon

    another latitude
   concave blue

butterfly trapped in your eyes

Land Outside
Land Inside
Travel-
the place they meet

Once on a walk
and it was raining
I cried for no other reason
than to have my tears
mix with the rain

Last night, I had the sea for brain.
Listen! Put your ear to mine
and hear the rush waves make.
Never two alike. Always the same.

I wait for your call, your voice
to come from my back,
the unknown door I carry
to open
and that voice to envelop me
like something before
music and words,
something before hands
and eyes,
something like the sea
because everything I don't know
is like the sea.
I only know I love you.
You'll tell me why

ALICE'S POEMS

Thoughts in the Park

How long have these pines
whispered to each other secrets?

A stone monument,
"Presented by The Ladies Improvement Club 1912"
I still hear the ladies gossiping in their starched aprons
2016 the ladies reappear, walk around the park, chatter
to one another
I want to listen to pine, live oak
The ladies wear sneakers and yoga pants
We are invited to free senior lunch, a John Wayne movie,
folk dance class

The drone of cars drowns out
the twitter of a small bird with crested head

I wonder about a block of cement cordoned off
with yellow caution tape

A curious pine branch dips down over it
Is it trying to protect or simply asking questions?

The huge pine displays its rough bark in art patterns
It does not know about Georgia O'Keefe
It will not take a selfie

Homeless

I am sure that man in the park
with blankets and shopping cart
once had a home where he could dream
What cruel tornado blew it away?
Dream on, man. Dream on.

If you could make your own thought, visions
Could they not go out
and make a home for you?

Who smashed that man's dream
that he can now find
no place to live?
What sort of death
before death is this?

Saxophone player squawks for no one
and everyone
The live oak drops tiny invisible tips

Dry water gulley
lined with stones
Pine trees lean towards it
looking for water

People wander in and out
of the Senior Center
Their votes placed, eyes to the ground
Huge pines wonder
why someone must be in charge

Even the Indians had government
I would prefer to be ruled
by that ancient benevolent pine tree

Car alarm horn
You compete with sparrows
and that saxophone squawk
Who will notate this cacophony?

Sparrow

Homeless sparrow
your chirps are hidden
behind the car horn alarm
and my old thoughts
No one has taught you
to phone home

Sweet, sparrow, you do not need
to make cheerful conversation
with aging relatives or sip cognac
stare into a crackling fire
write poems

Little sparrow, you are not worried
about the hot sun
and that there are no clouds
to cool you on your old ladies' walk
around the park

Tiny singer sparrow, you do not need
to memorize your music for the performance
You do not care
if we listen to you or not

Stay with the Trees

who pose and smile
though we do not notice
They will never psychoanalyze you
or tell you who you are
or whom you must become

Talk to the trees,
they do not care if they are famous poets
Their poems are hidden inside their bark
I press my ear to hear

Sing to the trees
They will love you
for drowning out the sirens,
the loud honking of car alarms

Run and sing while the trees' branches
dance with wind music,
never concerned about beginnings
or endings, flowing life rhythm
without a single thought

Little Fly

will you alight upon me?
this poem
might be your invention

Where was I
when the trees last spoke?
Or are they speaking now
and I cannot hear?
Towering pine
spreads wide branches
dropping smiles
There are no words

Little boy running
doesn't need a playground,
swings or slides
He has that magic stick
and all the pine needles

The Lone Birch

looks out over the parking lot
at the huge grove of pines,
yearning for its mother and brothers
Is that why it turns brown?

Silent Park

No sirens
No horns honking
No screaming children
The old sax player
carves a song in the air

Two little dogs
One tall boy
walking them
Where is his chariot?

Yellow police tape
closes in a small cement circle
A forbidden ritual?
Ancient crime scene?

The park grass,
soft, warm and fragrant
I left the fleas home
on the cat

Thin pine needles
under my feet
Gnats hover
What are the old men saying
across the park?

"Hot coals"
shouts the sign
on the park BBQ
We try to get them glowing
with our eyes

Old scraggly tree leans
to speak to the giant pine
whispering secrets

Sweeping pine proudly
talks to the sky
ignores its gnarly toes
alligator bark

Industrious squirrels
run on tiny feet
Sad, homeless humans sit
like statues

The ambitious runner times herself
with a little machine, gauges her heartbeat
I sit on a bench, with an old pencil,
quietly exhaling a small poem

Mail truck eases itself
onto the roadway
unconcerned
with the weight of junk mail

The day so large
bright yellow and blue
Why can I only squeeze out
tiny poems?

Kind pines drop needles
a blanket to comfort
dry, crying earth

Bukowski Listening

What are those cigarette butts
whispering to each other about
in the dirty sand, those beer cans?
The old poet is listening

Monument

So solid and sad
Stones on a monument
Keeping death for us

Clover Poet

If that clover could scribble a poem
would it be an ode to a bee
or is will it brag about besting a boot?

14th Way to Look at a Blackbird
or How the Blackbird Looked Back
*   with respect to Wallace Stevens*

Call me crow
I glisten
My caw is loud and rough
I have never heard of the bawds of euphony

Before bees were bees
were they slivers of air?

Those succulents hugging ground
Care not for rain
Hold juicy stories inside

Cactus has no one to bite
entertains spiders
learns weaving and aerial dance

In ancient Greece
gods swooped and begat other gods
In Tujunga there are hawks

Apple

The apple on the ground
does it feel the wind?

Its thought only to lie there
and one must wish upon it,
the yellow glowing,
the ground soft after the rain
its seeds silent
to make nothing more
never concerned with waste

The apple on the ground
does it feel the wind?
the haste?

The Day

pulls itself together
and spreads itself out
with the sun and the wind
as clouds advance and retreat
as one breathes the sweet air
in and out
That loud voice close by condensing
thought to a point
then fading

The Fall Wind

rippling through my head
forming thoughts
like the apricots on that tiny tree
not yet blossoming

I must stop the wind
then draw it forth
Find myself
in the air

Three lines
to wish myself awake
thud of apples falling

Crow

caws for sweets
drops a shiny black feather
I praise him in a poem
Make him famous

Arithmetic

Who weighs the flower
at the end of tall, hollyhock stalk?
Who is measuring wind
pulling at butterfly wing?

Sitting Next to the Trash Can

I try to find a poem
Old sax man swearing
in between notes
he tries to find on the page

Electric Trees

Are you electric?
I ask the trees
Does your sap pulsate
with energy that zaps us alive
as we lean sideways
to breathe in your forever green?

Matisse & the Bird

"The air is so dry," says the bird
"I can cut it with my beak"
"Make a cut-out," says Matisse

Palm tree
has a long beard
Budget cuts

Back Home

I feel dry
look for an idea
in my crowded closet
find an old felt hat
I leave the door ajar

Elsa Frausto, who hails from Argentina and resides in Tujunga, is a bilingual poet and translator. She's been active in the local literary community since the 1980's participating in readings (Beyond Baroque, art galleries and libraries), producing cultural programs in Spanish (KPFK radio), editor of Lahoja and la-luciérnaga.com, a member of Chuparosa Writers, coordinator and host of Camelback Readings. Her work has appeared in many publications, among them Porte des Poetes, Hispanic L.A., Four Bilingual L.A. Poets, Spine Flower Blues, and in two chapbooks *South of You* and *Night Birds*, which she also edited. As Poet Laureate Of Sunland-Tujunga, she is active with the Village Poets and she coordinates and hosts the monthly series "Wide Open Reading".

Alice Pero's poetry has been published in many magazines including Nimrod, National Poetry Review, River Oak Review, Poet Lore, The Alembic, North Dakota Quarterly, The Griffin, and G.W. Review and the anthologies *Coiled Serpent* and *Wide Awake*. Her first book of poetry, *Thawed Stars*, was praised by Kenneth Koch as having "clarity and surprises." Pero is a teacher of poetry and a member of California Poets in the Schools. Ms. Pero is an accomplished flutist and founder of Windsong Players Chamber Ensemble. She created the reading series Moonday in 2002, which is now at The Flintridge Bookstore in La Cañada CA. The prolific Pero has created dialogue poems with over twenty-five poets. She has been a Sunland resident since 2006.

www.ingramcontent.com/pod-product-compliance
Lightning Source LLC
Chambersburg PA
CBHW032107040426
42449CB00007B/1214